# BOOST
# YOURSELF

# Dedication

I dedicate this book to any businesswomen, who feel stressed and overwhelmed, who may be feeling a little bit stuck or a little lost. I hope the Boost Yourself Journal brings you a little comfort, that it provides a safe place for you to get things of your chest, a place to reflect, set goals, manifest your dreams and move forward. There are lots of women here providing helpful tips and advice so please never feel alone, I'm here to help! If I can't, I'll know someone who can!

This journal is also dedicated to all the fabulous business women I have worked with since setting up Miss Digital Media. An extra special shout out goes to my fellow Digital Women! Thank you all for inspiring me, supporting me and collaborating with me! Together we have achieved so many great things!

# Contents Page

MiSS DiGiTAL MEDIA

# Introduction

**W**elcome to the Boost Yourself Journal. I hope that this journal helps you to Boost Yourself and your business in what ever way you need it to.

My name is Beckie Sanderson I am a branding designer, online marketing and publishing specialist. I set up my business Miss Digital Media in 2019 after being made redundant. Since then I have had the pleasure of working with such a diverse range of businesswomen, who are all at different stages in their business journey. Many are experts in their fields, whether that be as a mindset coach, a health and wellbeing consultant or product and service based businesses.

There are many things that myself and all these women have in common, we all work very hard, we are all ambitious, passionate and determined to succeed. Many of us have children and some of us struggle more than others to juggle our personal lives, our own well being and self care as well as continually developing our businesses.

The Boost Yourself Journal is for you ladies, a tool that you can use to help 'Boost Yourself' when you need it, a place for you to practice mindfulness, gratitude and reflection, to record your achievements, to help you on the difficult days and to keep you on track with your personal and business goals.

But there are so many different reasons that I wanted to create this journal. Initially, I wanted to develop this journal for myself and for my clients to use. I found that many other journals didn't have all the bits in that I wanted in the format that I wanted it! Which is why I decided to create my own! At times I feel overwhelmed, and stuck as a busy business owner and mum. I have always struggled with my own limiting beliefs and crippling imposter syndrome, especially in my business. I know I'm not the only one. I know that many of my clients feel the same way. Although we each have our own challenges and personal issues to face, the common thing is the sense of overwhelm and a feeling of being stuck.

In my typical fashion I always want to help others, often putting others before myself. This is especially true in my business - and unsurprisingly that is true for many of my clients too. I'm an empath so naturally I attract other empaths and also those who really need my help. The thing with that is that I take on the stress and worry of others, while continuing to overlook my own needs. I really struggle with my own self care, just to take some time out and look after myself can be a real challenge for me.

I've worked with lots of coaches and done lots of work on my own personal development, learning about gratitude, mindfulness, limiting beliefs, mindset and manifesting. As I said, I've used many other journals, planners and notebooks to help plan my diary, the layout of the pages helps me to use time blocking techniques, set goals and pages to reflect, journal and doodle, but I've found them so frustrating! The books I've used either didn't have not enough prompts or too many prompts, or they didn't have right sections for the information I want to track and record. This left me feeling annoyed at myself that I haven't kept up with daily journaling in the dated planners, or that there wasn't enough space to write, mindmap and doodle or a place to track my mood and self care.

Instead, I wanted the flexibility to journal on some days and not others, to track my mood and self care, or some days to focus on gratitude and reflection or to set goals, I wanted to have some space for mind-mapping, drawing, doodling, sketching and colouring. I wanted all of the best bits in the other journals but I wanted to do it my way! Luckily I design books so it was a no-brainer! The idea for my 'Boost Yourself' Journal was born!

I felt really inspired by Nikki Sawyer, who has a fantastic Facebook group for anxious mums called 'From Fear to Freedom'. Nikki is a very supportive and creative person who advocates creative journaling which is something that I really feel drawn to do, to reflect on my day, as a stress reliever and the creative process of drawing, colouring, doodling and crafting. When I do take the time to do these things especially colouring and doodling, I find that it really helps to calm my mind and fulfil my creative desire. However I've really struggled to allow myself permission or the time to journal. Which is why I'd asked Nikki Sawyer, who I've dubbed the 'Queen of Journaling' to share her tips and wise words about the benefits of journaling., Nikki also suggested that I include a permission slip in this journal - which Nikki explains more about in her foreword.

There were other reasons for me wanting to create the Boost Yourself Journal too. As a book designer and specialist in self publishing I want to create books and lots of them! For myself and my clients. I wanted to demonstrate how easily a book can be put together and published to generate a passive income, as a tool to generate leads, and boost brand visibility.

In addition to that, I've always wanted to create colouring books and note books. I love pattern design and illustration, and I dream of creating designs and self publishing lots of low content books. It has been one of my goals for over a year now to create a colouring book. However my self sabotaging ways and limiting beliefs have prevented me from doing that. During a zoom call with my client Faye Cox - a mindset and confidence coach, we got talking about my goal to create a colouring book over a year ago. She asked 'Well what's stopping you?' I reeled off a list of reasons which I realised as soon as the words left my lips were just a whole lot of excuses and my usual self sabotaging ways where my imposter likes to limit and destroy my confidence, self belief and creativity. Faye set me the challenge to create my colouring book within two months. I soon realised that I it would take a long time to create all of the illustrations. So, I decided to take a different approach, rather than create a full on colouring book, instead I would create the Boost Yourself Journal as a low content book with a few colouring pages and elements in - a more manageable, comfortable and achievable project! I have already published my first ebook - Boost

Your Brand with Books which is available on Amazon and I have plans to publish moreYour books as part of a series including 'Boost Your Brand' (which is currently being written) and 'Boost Your Visibility' etc. So the Boost Yourself Journal will be a great addition to the series.

It has proved to be a really therapeutic, enjoyable and valuable project both personally and professionally. However it has taken a lot more time than I anticipated in pulling all of the content together. Initially I posted in my Facebook group to request that the ladies in my group send me their 'Boost Yourself' tips for business owners relating to their area of business and expertise, this offered a free advertising opportunity for them and their businesses. I was so happy to receive such a positive response to the idea of the Boost Yourself Journal, and I am so pleased that I decided to take the different approach and to get others involved in contributing their tips and expertise. I'm so happy with how it has all come together!

I'm also proud of myself that I've taken a positive step in creating my next book - now a colouring book feels more achievable for me! And I'm really proud to have created the Boost Yourself Journal that I hope will help others as much as I know it will help me, I feel so passionate and connected to it after this process. As I sit here writing this now, I am visualising myself doodling and practising mindfulness, gratitude and manifestation, and continuing to work on boosting my self confidence, self belief and creativity. Hopefully it will also help me in overcoming the limiting beliefs and imposter syndrome which have held me back and kept me stuck.

I'd love you to share your feedback on how the Boost Yourself Journal has helped you, please can you leave a review on Amazon, on my Facebook page or in my group:

Facebook page: **@Missdigitalmedia**
Facebook group: **@missdigitalmediaclassroom**

Thank you

Beckie Sanderson
Branding designer, Online Marketing & Publishing Specialist
Miss Digital Media
www.missdigitalmedia.co.uk

# MiSS DiGiTAL MEDiA

# Foreword - By Nikki Sawyer The Queen of Journaling!

Hello! I am Nikki Sawyer, I'm so excited to collaborate with Beckie in writing this foreword for the Boost Yourself Journal. Beckie has created a fabulous tool that will help many businesswomen, I think you are going to love it!

Just to give you a little bit of background information about myself and why Beckie has dubbed me 'The Queen of Journaling!'

I'm a busy business owner and a mum of three. After I had my third child I suffered from postnatal depression and very high anxiety. Through years of battling and high medication, I soon realised that nothing was going to change unless I started to make things different for myself. However, I found myself. I started at the beginning and permitted myself to work on ME! Not the kids, hubby, house, or career, just ME!

Since then, I have been on a life changing journey, an adventure of my own! I have built up a business that allows me to help other mums who feel stuck in the cycle of anxiety. I have created a place of support, help, and guidance called 'Sentient'. Sentient means to feel in Latin. So many of us are too scared to feel, we don't allow ourselves to do it. Journaling is a huge element of my support for others. I journal myself daily, it is my go-to when feeling stressed, anxious, or unsure, I paint, draw, colour and write. A busy foggy head does not provide good choices. Journaling can help you break free from the cycle of anxiety by tweaking your thought process. Once you do this your behaviour changes which will then create a reality you are much happier in, and with far less anxiety involved.

The Boost Yourself Journal is a fabulous tool to practice and implement change to 'Boost Yourself' and your business. It provides a journey of permission, acceptance and growth. A safe space for self-development, goal setting, reflection, and implementation. It has been created in a way that will allow you to take it at your own pace, and you'll have FUN doing it! Change starts with you, no one is going to do this for you. I think the moment you acknowledge and realise this, is the moment when you begin to move forward and rule your world!

## So why should you journal?

The mind doesn't know what's real and what's not until you tell it! How amazing is that! So when feeling consumed with negativity and anxiety, it's a clear-cut sign that we have some bad behaviour habits going on. When wanting to feel happier, less anxious, and positive your journal is a key tool in making this happen. Your thought process creates your behaviour, your behaviour creates your reality. If you constantly feed your thoughts on the bad stuff, you are not going to feel great, let's face it!

You can start your journey of change but miss all the positive small steps you make along the way. When you journal, you log them and have a place to turn to for reflection and validation that what you are doing is working. This is what the unconscious mind wants, evidence! So why do so many of us NOT journal? Limiting beliefs and blocks is the main reason.

## My journaling tips

**Give yourself permission:** Complete the permission slip and allow yourself to take the time to journal. Many ladies feel their time should be spent doing other things and not writing or creating or putting themselves first. This is wrong, stop the doubt and sign away, when it's done, you can begin guilt-free. Also allow yourself to be flexible, imperfect (perfection is not real). Time block Journaling into your evening. Just 10 minutes to start and find your flow.

**Be consistent:** Journal every day (or as regularly as you can), 3 positives from your day. It could be anything from self-care time, kids went to school without a fight, you found peace with yourself throughout the day, you achieved what you wanted in your business or perhaps just focus on what you HAVE got, and what you CAN do, write one of those elements in if you are struggling to start.

**Be accountable:** A new habit takes 21-28 days to create and stick to. If you are not consistent it's not going to work. The aim here is to get you thinking positively and break free from the negative self-talk and anxiety. Journaling is to become your new self-care, and self-help routine. If it's not working, you haven't committed.

**Tweak it:** The Boost Yourself Journal's 'Today I' prompt allows you to start tweaking! Tweak how you talk to yourself, view yourself, love yourself, and first and foremost permit yourself to do all of the above.

**Get creative:** Enjoy colouring Beckie's illustrations and getting creative!

Are you ready, to start using The Boost Yourself Journal as your new safe space to find yourself and put yourself first? DO IT, you've got this!

You can also work with me, and I can help you to make a start, implement and commit to journaling.

I wish you all the best on your journaling adventure.

Nikki xxx

**Get in touch:**
www.nikkisawyer.co.uk
Join my Facebook group: feartofreedomformums

# Your Permission Slip

I _____

give myself permission to journal,

create and be grateful in a way that is

bad, messy, incomplete, strange or unplanned.....

from now until always.

Signed: _____

Dated: _____

# How to use this Journal

The Boost Yourself Journal is set out with undated, lined and blank pages, for you to practice journaling, to get stuff out of your head on to paper, you can practice daily gratitude, reflection and manifestation, set goals, or plan out your business projects. Firstly complete your permission slip, the mission & purpose and the ideal client exercises. These will help to boost yourself and your business!

You can use each page as you like, there is no right or wrong way to do it! Use the blank pages to mind map your ideas, doodle, sketch and colour away your stress.

Each left hand page starts with the Miss Digital Media icon and 'Today I' prompt. You can use the icon as a mood tracker by adding a smiley face or sad face, or you can just doodle on it! Have fun with her, draw little outfits, hats or fill with patterns and colour her in! Whatever floats your boat!

The idea of the 'Today I' prompt is that you can take it in any direction that you want each day you use it - for example:

# Today I...

feel overwhelmed because...
feel stressed because...
feel great because...
feel proud because...
feel like celebrating because...
am grateful for...
am reflecting on...
am setting a goal to...
am manfiesting...

Each left hand page also features 'Boost Yourself Tips' from a diverse mix of businesswomen who are sharing their tips and expertise on branding, business development, marketing, mindset, confidence, fashion & style, health & wellbeing, healthy eating tips, meditation and breathing exercises plus much more.

There is a business directory is at the back of the journal, if you would like any further support and information from any of the business women featured.

I hope that this journal really does help you to 'Boost Yourself' and your business!

# Mission & Purpose

Your business purpose is the reason or reasons why your business exists, whereas your business mission is about what you do and who for. Doing this excercise will help to boost yourself, your business and your brand. Also it can help you to gain some clarity and remind you why you do what you do, and why you are so good at it!

**MISSION & PURPOSE:** The business purpose is the reason or reasons why your business exists, whereas the mission is about what you do and for who.

**WHO:** Who are you? Who are your customers? Who do you help?

**WHY:** Why do you do what you do? Why do you love it? Why do people need your products and services? Why should people buy from you?

**WHAT:** What do you do? What products and services do you offer? What problems do you solve for your customers? What difference or transfor mation do you provide for your customers?

**HOW:** How do your products and services help to solve a problem or transform the lives of your customers and clients? How do you provide these services? How much do your products and services cost?

**WHERE:** Where do you operate your business? Where do you sell your products and services? Where do you sell online? Where do you promote online and on what platforms? Where do you reach your clients?

Do you know your Mission & Purpose in your business? The why, who, what, where and how of your business?

In the sections below write out your mission and purpose and the why, who, what, where and how of your business. The information you write here can be used in your marketing and promotions and to help you to fill in your ideal client worksheet on the next page. If you feel stuck with this try creating a mind map using the prompts below.

## YOUR MISSION & PURPOSE:

## WHO:

## WHY:

## WHAT:

## HOW:

## WHERE:

# Are you attracting your ideal customers & clients?

**B**usiness owners need be clear on who their ideal clients or customers are, whether that is selling business to business or business to consumer. The ideal client excersise can be used for any type of business such as sole traders, business partnerships or MLM businesses who may have either product and or a serviced based businesses.

Going through this exercise will help you to define your ideal customer, their characteristics, likes and dislikes, what their jobs and income are and where they are online. I am sure that you will find this an interesting and productive exercise.

You should carry out research and fill in the sections with the relevant information, you may need to return to this several times as you will have revelations and ideas that will come to you during the process.

## Identify the answers to these questions:

- What do you know about your ideal client?
- What problem are you solving for your client or customer?
- What solutions can you provide?
- What products and services can you offer to solve the problem?
- Who uses them and why?
- How does that transform things for them?
- What does that transformation look and sound like?
- What hobbies and interests do they have?
- Where are they online/offline?
- How are you going to reach them?

Once the ideal client sheet is complete you can write your ideal client scenario which depicts an ideal customer story and how you will solve their problems with your product and services.

It will be helpful to give your ideal client a name, personality, and information about them that helps you build your ideal client's persona. It might even be based on one of your real clients, or it could be a fictional person.

You may find that these will be a great source of creating content which you will be able to use in your marketing, social media, website and blogs.

# Ideal Client Worksheet

**CUSTOMER PROFILE:** Who and where are your customers? What characteristics and information do you know about them?

Gender:
Age:
Salary:
Location:

**CLIENT TYPE:** Are your customers, consumers or business owners? Do they provide products or services to other businesses or to consumers? Are they a new or established business? What do they do? Who are their customers? What demographic are they in? What job do they do, what type of personality do they have?

**PROBLEM:** Describe why your customers have a problem? What do they need or desire? What do they want to change? How does it makes them feel?

**SOLUTION:** Who can you provide solutions for? What solutions can you provide? Why will this help? Where will you deliver this service? How does this makes them feel?

**PRODUCTS:** What products can you offer to solve the problem? Who uses them and why? How wiil it make a difference to their lives?

**SERVICES:** What services can you offer? Who uses them and why? How does that transform things for them? What does that transformation look and sound like?

**HOBBIES & INTERESTS**
What hobbies and interests do your customers have? What books do they read? What subjects are the interested in? What programmes do they watch? What do you have in common with them?

**ONLINE/OFFLINE ACTIVITY:** Describe where your customers are online/offline. How and where can you find them? What places, shops and websites, social platforms and groups are they using? What do they talk about or do?

**EMAIL SIGN UP:** Whose email newsletters do they sign up for and why? What value are they getting: information, vouchers special offers, jobs or learning?

**EVENTS:** What online/offline events do they go to and how you can reach them at those events?

**KEYWORDS:** What key words and google search phrases do your customers use? What problems or questions might they ask? How can reach them with these key words and phrases? SEO/ Blogs, Hashtags? Ads?

# Your Ideal Client Worksheet

CUSTOMER PROFILE:                    CLIENT TYPE:

Gender:
Age:
Salary:
Locations:

PROBLEM:                             ONLINE/OFFLINE ACTIVITY:

EMAIL SIGN UP:

SOLUTION:

EVENTS:

PRODUCTS:

HOBBIES &
INTERESTS

KEYWORDS:

SERVICES:

# Ideal Client Scenario

**Y**ou should put yourself in your customers shoes to really understand how you can help to make them feel better, to help them with the things they might be struggling with or how you can help them to achieve their goals.

Every business will have its unique selling points and a different customer base. So you should try to include these different aspects when writing your scenario.

You may find it helpful to create more than one scenario with slight variations which will appeal to different people and situations, or more specifically to fit the different products or services you offer.

Once you have completed these, you can use them to start developing content for your marketing and promotions. As an example, see Miss Digital Media's ideal client scenario below.

**Please get in touch:** if you need help to develop your own ideal client info sheets, or to give some feedback on how you got on at Miss Digital Media's Facebook page using the HashTags **#BoostYourselfJournal #Idealclient**

## My ideal client scenario

My ideal client is Sam. Sam is a self employed Business Coach and mum of 2, she is aged 40 and has a salary of approximately £25-35k. Sam lives in the Midlands UK, and her customers are worldwide. Sam has a well established business and customer base, she needs help to rebrand her business and monthly support with her online marketing. Sam is not at all creative, so really struggles with the time, creativity and technical skills to create engaging content for her website and social media. Sam has developed a business training programme and has written a book but doesn't have a clue about self publishing books or how to generate leads to sign up for her programme. Sam needs help to scale up her business and create conversions fast.

Miss Digital Media will provide logo and branding design services, and monthly support to design online marketing graphics and update Sam's website and blog.

Miss Digital Media will also provide design, formatting and publishing services to self publish Sam's book and ebook on Amazon.

As well as providing monlthy 1-2-1 training and support to develop Sam's content plan and schedule social media posts, create a landing page, email sign up form and set up automated email newsletters and email marketing campaigns.

Miss Digital Media's solution's are just what Sam needs to build her brand. Outsourcing the creative and technical work and learning new skills all help to remove the stress and overwhelm of managing her online marketing, and will help to free up her time so she can do what she does best.

# Your Ideal Client Scenario

Use the information you have gathered in completing the Ideal client worksheet and Miss Digital Media's ideal client scenario to help you to write your own ideal client scenario. Giving your ideal client a name can really help you to visualise them.

# BOOST YOURSELF

# Today I...

**Boost Yourself Tip:**

**Nikki Sawyer - Sentient - www.nikkisawyer.co.uk**

*"I highly recommend defogging a messy head with a beautiful journal. There are many ways to journal. You can journal for positivity, and shift in mindset and you can journal to get things out on paper. Once you actually see it, it jumps into your conscious mind and you can work on moving forward and clearing the blocks. Journaling is also a huge element of self-care time. Self-care time is key to moving forward and positivity."*

# Today I...

**Boost Yourself Tip:**

**Beckie Sanderson - Miss Digital Media**
**www.missdigitalmedia.co.uk**

*"If you have a talent, a skill, a story or a concept to share,
there is no better place for it than in a book!"*

# Today I...

**Boost Yourself Tip:**

**Becky Clarke - Tarot Reader and Astrologer**
**www.thebeckyclarke.co.uk**

*"Record yourself repeating a few affirmations about yourself or business for a couple of minutes. Play it to yourself every day for 30 days or until you believe them".*

# Today I...

**Boost Yourself Tip:**

**Beckie Sanderson - Miss Digital Media**
**www.missdigitalmedia.co.uk**

*"What does your logo say about you? Does it give the right impression of your business? Does it represent your brand well? Does it appeal to your ideal clients? As a business owner, there are many aspects to consider in creating logo's and branding, such as budget, functionality and design. When investing, ensure that your branding assests are fit for purpose and provide a return on the investment."*

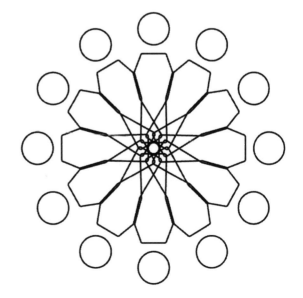

# Today I...

**Boost Yourself Tip:**

**Esther Ocampo - The Monday Morning Marketing Podcast**
**www.themondaymorningmarketing.com**

*"Repurpose your content. Turn your podcast into a blog,
a video into numerous social media posts - the list is endless."*

# Today I...

# Today I...

**Boost Yourself Tip:**

**Halima Keshav (Mindful Coach/Reflexologist)**
**Beautiful Sole Therapies - www.beautifulsole.co.uk**

*"Breathing - Take a few minutes to notice the ebb & flow of your breathe.*
*The rise and fall of your belly. Spending 5 minutes a day breathing deeply*
*can help you focus more clearly."*

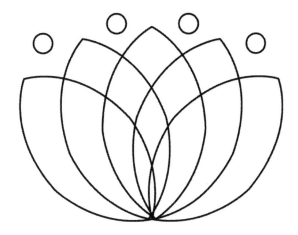

# Today I...

**Boost Yourself Tip:**

**Beckie Sanderson - Miss Digital Media**
**www.missdigitalmedia.co.uk**

*"Building a brand takes time, it doesn't happen over night."*

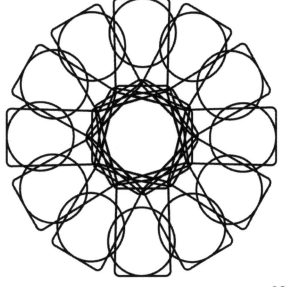

# Today I...

**Boost Yourself Tip:**

**Katie Spreadbury - OrangeSheep Research Ltd**
**www.orangesheepresearch.co.uk**

*"Never make assumptions about what is going on for your ideal clients. They do not have your knowledge, expertise, or experience... you need to ask questions about what is going on in their world and show up with a solution to the problems they think they have, irrespective of what you know is really going on underneath."*

# Today I...

**Beckie Sanderson - Miss Digital Media**
**www.missdigitalmedia.co.uk**

*"Do your hashtag research on your business niche and ideal clients,
Search and follow those hashtags on instagram. Facebook, Twitter and LinkedIn to see
who is using and engaging with them on those platforms. Create hashtags lists, and
keep them as a note file on your mobile phone or computer to make it quick and easy to
copy and paste into your posts."*

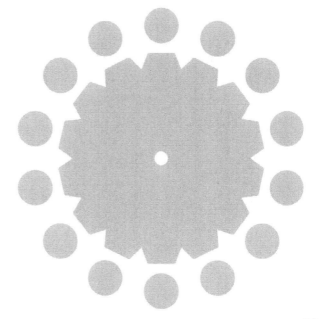

# Today I...

**Boost Yourself Tip:**

**Nisha Harichandran - Bohem Notes**
**www.bohemiancrossing.blog**

*"Pour it out. Have fun. Play. Create. Ideate."*

# Today I...

**Boost Yourself Tip:**

**Beckie Sanderson - Miss Digital Media**
**www.missdigitalmedia.co.uk**

*"Boost Your Skills, Boost Your Brand, Boost Yourself!"*

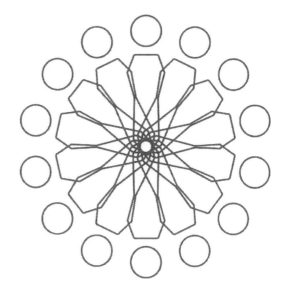

# Today I...

# Today I...

# Today I...

---

## Boost Yourself Tip:

**Jen Parker - Job Done Digital**
**www.jobdonedigital.com**

*"Once you publish your ad hold your nerve!*
*The algorithm needs time to learn and understand peoples behaviours.*
*Every change you make sets the algorithm back to the start of the learning journey so*
*hold out at least 3-5 days before making any adjustments."*

# Today I...

---

## Boost Yourself Tip:

**Beckie Sanderson - Miss Digital Media**
**www.missdigitalmedia.co.uk**

*"Get clear about your ideal client - who are they, why they need your products and services, what problems can you solve for them, how can you transform things for them, and where can you find them online and offline."*

# Today I...

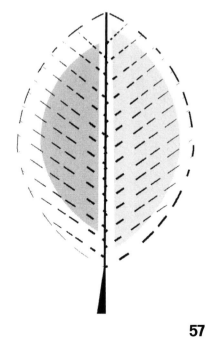

# Today I...

## Boost Yourself Tip:

**Beckie Sanderson - Miss Digital Media**
**www.missdigitalmedia.co.uk**

*"Repurposing your existing content, videos, blogs, posts, and graphics helps to develop your brand consistency and communicate your key messages across different platforms, where you can interact with and grow your audience, create a community, and build the 'like, know and trust factor."*

# Today I...

**Boost Yourself Tip:**

**Yuki Lam - Cultivate Life**
**www.cultivatethelife.com**

*"Eat the rainbow. Eat as many colors as you can. Keeping your foods diverse, is better for health and Oh, makes food so much more fun and pretty!"*

# Today I...

**Boost Yourself Tip:**

**Beckie Sanderson - Miss Digital Media**
**www.missdigitalmedia.co.uk**

*"Think about what people and businesses you could collaborate with. What audiences could you reach and help? What projects could you get involved with that fit well or complement your brand and its products and services?"*

# Today I...

# Today I...

**Boost Yourself Tip:**

**Beckie Sanderson - Miss Digital Media**
**www.missdigitalmedia.co.uk**

*"Email marketing is the perfect place to boost your brand visibility. As such, building customer mailing lists are a great way to grow and nurture your audience.."*

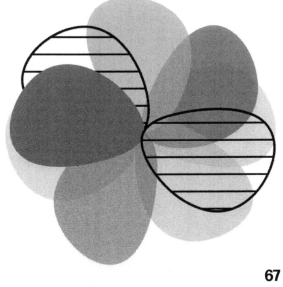

# Today I...

**Boost Yourself Tip:**

**Chris Melvile - Transform with Chris M**
**www.transformwithchrism.com**

*"These three questions move you from a negative, fixed mindset to a growth one fast.
What small action can I take to move just one step forward, is the challenge I'm facing
here to hinder my progress or show me ways to grow and today am I going to allow life
to happen to me or through me?"*

# Today I...

**Boost Yourself Tip:**

**Beckie Sanderson - Miss Digital Media**
**www.missdigitalmedia.co.uk**

*"Doing your research is the key to success in identifying your audience niche and clarifying the unique selling points of your business. Once you have this nailed, getting your brand visible to the right customers becomes a whole lot easier!"*

# Today I...

**Boost Yourself Tip:**

**Samantha Slater - Time & Money Coach**
**www.samanthajaneslater.com**

*"Value yourself and value your time.
Because when you have those values, money will flow."*

# Today I...

**Boost Yourself Tip:**

**Beckie Sanderson - Miss Digital Media**
**www.missdigitalmedia.co.uk**

*"Content planning helps to build consistency across your online marketing, blogs, social media, and email marketing channels. It enables you to be productive with your time, money, and resources and will help you to implement your marketing strategy, i.e the what, where, when, why, and to whom you should publish your content."*

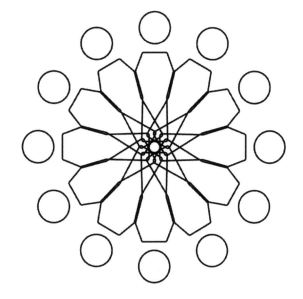

# Today I...

**Boost Yourself Tip:**

**Melanie Boylan - STOMP Social Media Training Ltd**
**www.stomp.ie**

*"Brand Persona and Tone of Voice actually help sway how people connect
and relate with you. Well worth looking into if you plan to have more
than one person managing your Social Media Profiles."*

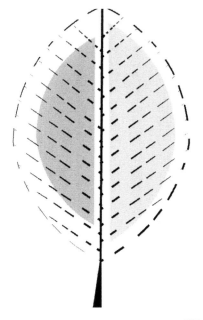

# Today I...

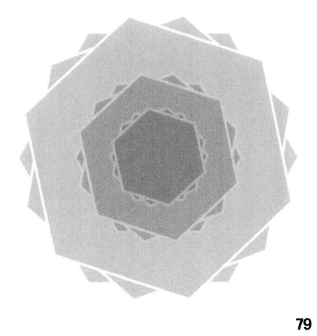

# Today I...

## Boost Yourself Tip:

**Jane Singleton - Jane Singleton Wellbeing**
**www.janesingletonreflexology.co.uk**

*"Don't under-estimate the power of taking (even what may seem like) tiny steps towards nurturing your wellbeing. Focus on 'just one thing' at a time - no matter how big or small - because before you know it that small thing becomes a new routine. Then celebrate, and repeat. All the little steps really do add up and make a difference to your wellbeing."*

# Today I...

# Today I...

## Boost Yourself Tip:

**Bridget Daley - Parents in Biz**
**www.parentsinbiz.co.uk**

*"Don't be one of those people who sit on the sidelines
and watch everyone else succeed and get the results you want.
You are worthy, You are deserving
And yes, you CAN do it!"*

# Today I...

_____

_____

_____

_____

_____

_____

_____

_____

_____

_____

_____

_____

_____

_____

_____

_____

_____

_____

**Boost Yourself Tip:**

**Beckie Sanderson - Miss Digital Media**
**www.missdigitalmedia.co.uk**

_"Self-publishing isn't just for authors - You or anyone can be an author! There are so many opportunities for everyone, whatever your niche! For example, if you're a mindset, confidence, or business coach. Whether you're a consultant, or an expert in your field, a specialist, a trainer, or an advisor. If you're a creative writer, photographer, illustrator, or artist, there's a book format and audience for you!"_

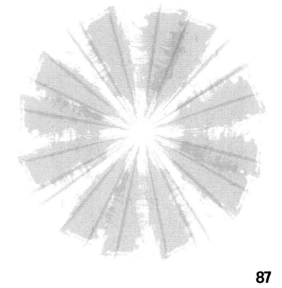

# Today I...

**Boost Yourself Tip:**

**Rachel Whiteside-Blaxter - Mindfulness Financial Planning**
**www.mindfulnessfp.co.uk**

*"Understand what self-limiting beliefs may be holding you back,
what assumptions you may make and how that can affect your financial decisions."*

# Today I...

# Today I...

**Boost Yourself Tip:**

**Lynn Rees - Virtual Assistant**
**www.lynnreesva.co.uk**

*"Outsource what you deteste doing, what you don't understand,
isn't going to give you the end result, or that can help you save or make money."*

# Today I...

**Boost Yourself Tip:**

**Beckie Sanderson - Miss Digital Media**
**www.missdigitalmedia.co.uk**

*"Boost your brand with books and eBooks - Books and eBooks can be used in many different ways to leverage your business to: establish yourself as an expert in your field, reach a broader audience with your programmes, share knowledge, and personal stories, add value to your existing customers or course delegates, to attract your ideal customers and help build the like, know, and trust factor."*

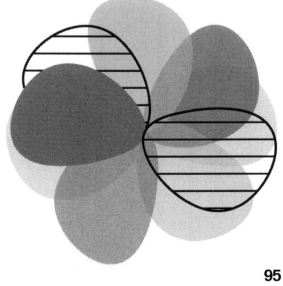

# Today I...

**Boost Yourself Tip:**

**Magdalena Kuraczowska - FAB Consulting Agency**
**www.femaleandbusiness.com - www.womenwhocowork.ie**

*""Feeling FAB everyday is to Be BRAVE, Be FAB and Be MORE. To truly shine and thrive online you first need to know your WHY, feel aligned with your vision! Take ownership of your achievements, speaking openly about who you are and how you can help others. No one can do this better than you - because YOU are the one that shines more than 1000 stars."*

# Today I...

_____
_____
_____
_____
_____
_____
_____
_____
_____
_____
_____
_____
_____
_____
_____
_____
_____
_____
_____
_____

**Boost Yourself Tip:**

**Beckie Sanderson - Miss Digital Media**
**www.missdigitalmedia.co.uk**

_"Please don't underestimate the power of SEO, keywords, and hashtags. They play a very important role in your brand visibility. Website SEO affects many things, including your position in a Google search listing and website traffic. Keywords also play a part in creating effective copy for your website and blogs and maximise your website's SEO, performance, and ability to attract your ideal clients and customers."_

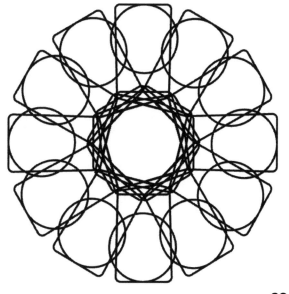

# Today I...

**Boost Yourself Tip:**

**Lisa Talbot - Lisa Talbot Personal Stylist.**
**www.lisatalbot.co.uk**

*"Always wear an item of clothing you love, gives you confidence and a positive mindset. Try to ensure a garment gives your body shape structure of some kind, it doesn't need to cling to give definition to your shape."*

# Today I...

**Boost Yourself Tip:**

**Beckie Sanderson - Miss Digital Media**
**www.missdigitalmedia.co.uk**

*"Do your research! It will help you make sure your marketing budget and strategy are effective, fit for purpose, and that it provides a return on investment."*

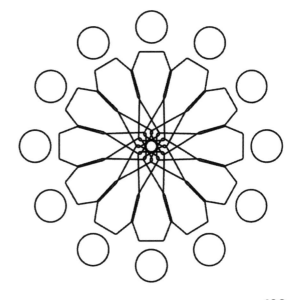

# Today I...

---

**Boost Yourself Tip:**

**Sarah Scarfe - Sarah Scarfe Marketing Ltd**
**www.sarahscarfe.com**

*"Check your tracking! Whatever tags you are using give them a check at least once a month to make sure everything is still in perfect working order. You're going to all of the effort so make sure it's measurable."*

# Today I...

## Boost Yourself Tip:

**Beckie Sanderson - Miss Digital Media**
**www.missdigitalmedia.co.uk**

*"Reuse and repurpose reviews, testimonials and feedback. Share the transformation you provide. Use your customers descriptions in your marketing content to help build the like, know and trust factor of your brand.."*

# Today I...

**Boost Yourself Tip:**

**Samantha Houghton - Memoir Mentor and Ghostwriter**
**www.samanthahoughton.co.uk**

*"Remember that effective content can be your thoughts, beliefs, advice, knowledge, insights and wisdom. It is all within you already, and it doesn't need to be complicated. Demonstrate passion and emotion and be YOU.."*

# Today I...

---

**Boost Yourself Tip:**

**Beckie Sanderson - Miss Digital Media**
**www.missdigitalmedia.co.uk**

*"Create big content such as books, eBooks, videos, courses, challenges, and activities to engage your audience, generate leads and help to build a passive or semi-passive income."*

# Today I...

**Boost Yourself Tip:**

**Soaad Patel - Ayeshas Attire**
**www.ayeshasattire.com**

*"If you dress well, you will feel good and when you feel good you're going to be productive in your day, which will help you to conquer that day's challenges."*

# Today I...

**Boost Yourself Tip:**

**Beckie Sanderson - Miss Digital Media**
**www.missdigitalmedia.co.uk**

*"Growing a community on any online platform takes a lot of time and effort. Nurturing and growing your audience takes real dedication. You will need to build rapport with your audience and engage with them so they can come to like, know and trust you. Having a well-engaged and growing community is priceless, because your audience is primed and ready for what you have to offer."*

114

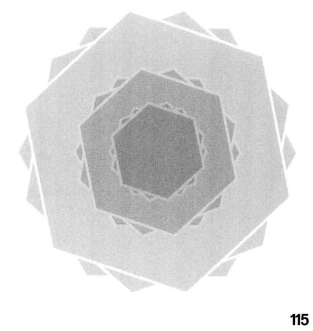

# Today I...

**Boost Yourself Tip:**

**Bettina Siddiqi - BusyB Solutions**
**www.busy-bsolutions.com**

*"To become more visible on LinkedIn it would help if you make your profile more searchable and make it stand out from the crowd, make sure you connect with your ideal clients and have a content strategy that resonates with your audience."*

# Today I...

**Boost Yourself Tip:**

**Beckie Sanderson - Miss Digital Media**
**www.missdigitalmedia.co.uk**

*"Make a great lead magnet that people will want to use. However, be aware that many won't even open the download, so don't give too much away for free – just a taster of the good stuff is enough!"*

# Today I...

_____

_____

_____

_____

_____

_____

_____

_____

_____

_____

_____

_____

_____

_____

_____

_____

_____

_____

_____

**Boost Yourself Tip:**

**Katie McGreal - Solas Relaxation agus Relax Kids**
**www.solasrelaxation.com**

*"When you're not feeling your work, when you're pushing and not enjoying what you're doing; stop. Stop and take a breath. Put two hands on your lower belly, straighten your back and take three slow deep breaths in through the nose and out through the mouth. You'll return to your work, to your life with a clearer head."*

# Today I...

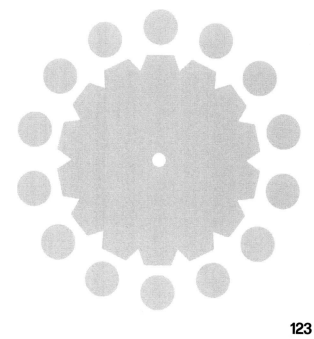

# Today I...

## Boost Yourself Tip:

**Ginny Marsh - Gorgeous You Coaching**
**www.gorgeousyoucoaching.com**

*"Wrte down 20 things you like/love about yourself, your appearance, your abilities, your personality, and your character. See if you can increase it to 50 or 100 positive things over time!"*

# Today I...

## Boost Yourself Tip:

**Beckie Sanderson - Miss Digital Media**
**www.missdigitalmedia.co.uk**

*"The Adobe Colour website and its clever tools to help you do a number of colourful things! Use the colour wheel to help generate complimentary colour palletes for your brand. Use the extract tool to extract colours from an image or logo and save them as colour a palette - this will also tell you the #hex code for your brand colours so you can use your brand colours on different platforms! See www.color.adobe.com."*

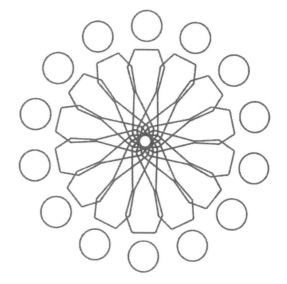

# Today I...

**Boost Yourself Tip:**

**Maya Saric - SharpShine Copy**
**Sharpshinecopy.com**

*"Put effort into creating a strong, you-thentic, and recognizable brand voice.
It'll help you stand out from the crowd."*

# Today I...

**Boost Yourself Tip:**

**Beckie Sanderson - Miss Digital Media**
**www.missdigitalmedia.co.uk**

*"Make it easy for your customers to give feedback.
Think about the processes and procedures you have in place for collecting customer
feedback and reviews. How you are going to use them to your marketing?"*

# Today I...

# Today I...

**Boost Yourself Tip:**

**Beckie Sanderson - Miss Digital Media**
**www.missdigitalmedia.co.uk**

*"Use customer feedback in your ongoing business development. How can you make improvements to your products and services? Think about how you can show your customers that you have listened and you are making a difference."*

# Today I...

# Today I...

**Boost Yourself Tip:**

**Beckie Sanderson - Miss Digital Media**
**www.missdigitalmedia.co.uk**

*"Use your insights and analytics data to review and develop your business,
online marketing, and customer experience."*

# Today I...

**Boost Yourself Tip:**

**Lisa Gillbe - Lisa Gillbe Style Consultancy**
**www.lisagillbestyle.com**

*"Take half a day to declutter your wardrobe. Getting rid of things you don't wear is cathartic and helps you to see the good stuff you have and to find outfits that make you feel good more easily."*

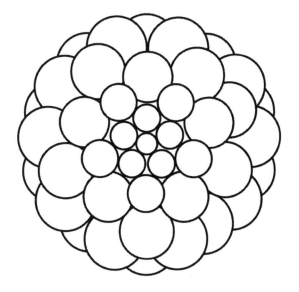

# Today I...

**Boost Yourself Tip:**

**Beckie Sanderson - Miss Digital Media**
**www.missdigitalmedia.co.uk**

*"Branding is about the design and promotion of a company, its products and services, and the methods used in marketing. Whether you have a business brand or a personal brand, at the core of your brand are the values, ideals, characteristics and personality traits of you and your company. These aspects as a whole are what make up your brand identity."*

# Today I...

## Boost Yourself Tip:

**Katie Earl - Fairy Blog Mother to coaches, consultants, and counsellors.**
**www.katie-earl-editing.co.uk**

*"Writing an effective blog for your business is about answering all the questions your audience has. Make sure you're covering common objections, questions, and mis-conceptions about your industry as part of your blog strategy."*

# Today I...

**Boost Yourself Tip:**

**Beckie Sanderson - Miss Digital Media**
**www.missdigitalmedia.co.uk**

*"Use technology and apps to automate your marketing and communications. Such as social media scheduling tools, automated email marketing, and messenger bots."*

# Today I...

**Boost Yourself Tip:**

**Carla Watkins - Business & Branding Photography**
**www.carlawatkins.com**

*"Have at least one glorious photo of yourself that you love, and keep it handy for sharing. It'll add to your confidence, and help you to share your business too!"*

# Today I...

_____

_____

_____

_____

_____

_____

_____

_____

_____

_____

_____

_____

_____

_____

_____

_____

_____

_____

**Boost Yourself Tip:**

**Beckie Sanderson - Miss Digital Media**
**www.missdigitalmedia.co.uk**

_"Buying branding is like buying shoes! We love our shoes, we feel excited about investing, they need to suit us and our personality, be comfortable to wear and be fit for purpose. We need to look after them, maintain them and sometimes repair them. We know it won't be our only pair of shoes, at some point we know we will need a new pair!" The same is true about investing, maintaining and repairing your business branding."_

# Today I...

**Boost Yourself Tip:**

**Faye Cox - Faye Cox Coaching**
**www.fayecoxcoaching.co.uk**

*"YOU ARE ENOUGH without all the stuff!."*

# Today I...

**Boost Yourself Tip:**

**Beckie Sanderson - Miss Digital Media**
**www.missdigitalmedia.co.uk**

*"Throughout the process of creating and developing a business or a personal brand, we have to think about so many different factors. A brand isn't just about the design of a company logo, and the colours used in marketing, it's so much more than that! It requires investment of time and money to continually develop. it."*

# Today I...

## Boost Yourself Tip:

**Kelly-Anne Geary - Tweak2Peak Lifestyle Coaching**
**www.tweak2peaklifestylecoaching.co.uk**

*"Get your steps up. Be creative if you struggle with this. Got a phone call to make? Walk and talk. Being active throughout the day is much better than exercising for 30-60 minutes and being sedentary for the rest of the day."*

# Today I...

_____

_____

_____

_____

_____

_____

_____

_____

_____

_____

_____

_____

_____

_____

_____

_____

_____

_____

_____

## Boost Yourself Tip:

**Beckie Sanderson - Miss Digital Media**
**www.missdigitalmedia.co.uk**

_"Keep reviewing - It's equally as important that as the company develops, that you continue to research, develop and review the success of your business and the brand, as you work to define your niche, grow your business and level up. Your brand should be viewed as a person, that needs to be nurtured, cared for and loved, just as much as the people behind the brand."_

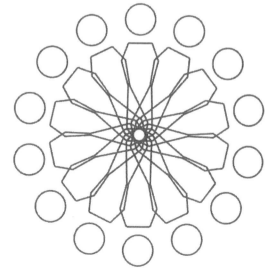

# Today I...

**Boost Yourself Tip:**

**Emma Whalley - Gossip Gals**
**www.gossipgalsnetworking.com**

*"My top tip to boost yourself is to go live! Confidence to go live can be an issue but consider all the great topics and advice you're holding back by not going live. Going live gets you more reach and builds relationships faster on social media."*

# Today I...

**Boost Yourself Tip:**

**Beckie Sanderson - Miss Digital Media**
**www.missdigitalmedia.co.uk**

*"Your brand identity forms the basis for all your communications, marketing, advertising and promotions. Your brand should be created to reach, attract and engage your ideal customers and clients and it should explain the who, why, what, where and how of your business."*

# Today I...

**Boost Yourself Tip:**

**Barbara Edwards - BeCoached**
**www.becoached.ie**

*"When you are in a stressful situation, take a long inhale for a count of 4 and exhale slowly for a count of 10. This will help you to ground yourself, reduces stress and help you refocus. The bonus is, no one knows you're doing it."*

# Today I...

**Boost Yourself Tip:**

**Beckie Sanderson - Miss Digital Media**
**www.missdigitalmedia.co.uk**

*"Consistency in your design, messaging, style and tone of voice are
the key aspects of boosting your brand and building brand visibility, awareness and
customer loyalty. Your customers perception and experience of your brand
will influence its reputation, good or bad."*

# Today I...

---

**Boost Yourself Tip:**

**Francesca Wynn - Network Inspired**
**www.network-inspired.co.uk**

*"When you first start out in business, have a business model typed / written out and have clear goal(s) in mind ie the purpose for your business, so you can provide this information, especially if you are looking for advice / support as a new business."*

# Today I...

**Boost Yourself Tip:**

**Beckie Sanderson - Miss Digital Media**
**www.missdigitalmedia.co.uk**

*"Branding should evolve - As our businesses evolve our brand should too, in a gradual and organic way."*

# Today I...

**Boost Yourself Tip:**

**Lisa Lomas - Lisa Lomas Therapies Community**
**Instagram: @lisalomastherapies**

*"To boost yourself, get some of your favourite pure essential oil, your nose knows, so let it pick. Take 30 seconds and add 1 drop to the palm of your hands, rub to warm the oil, cup over you're nose and mouth, and breathe deeply for that 30 seconds. I love to use doterra balance to start off with in the morning. Perfect."*

# Today I...

---

**Boost Yourself Tip:**

**Beckie Sanderson - Miss Digital Media**
**www.missdigitalmedia.co.uk**

*"Brand Visibility Do's - Get yourself out there - Feel the fear and do it anyway! Get confident on camera, making videos and taking selfies. Create great content to attract and engage your ideal clients. Networking and promotion is key, find your people - grow your tribe. Be Authentic - Be yourself to build the Like, Know, and Trust factor with potential clients. Remember we are all on our own journey and all at different stages."*

# Today I...

**Boost Yourself Tip:**

**Faye Cox - Faye Cox Coaching**
**www.fayecoxcoaching.co.uk**

*"Your mind is always listening - so be mindful what you're telling it!"*

# Today I...

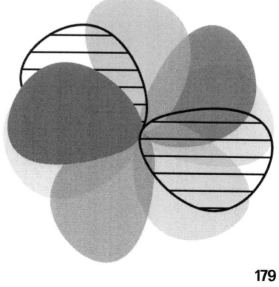

# Today I...

**Boost Yourself Tip:**

**Annabelle Antão-Bithrey - House of Colour Longfield**
**Instagram @styleandconfidence**

*"As an image consultant I would encourage you to get your colours and style analysed. This knowledge will last you a lifetime. I also encourage you to embrace your accessories wear necklaces, statement earrings and gorgeous scarves that suit your body architecture. They really do transform an outfit!"*

# Today I...

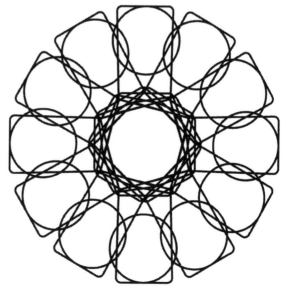

# Today I...

**Boost Yourself Tip:**

Sheree Owen - Sales Strategist
www.shereeowensalesstrategist.co.uk

*"Sales confidence comes knowing and believing that you have a valuable solution to offer to your ideal client who is out there. Creating great relationships where know, like and trust can be built which enables you to close sales with confidence and grow your business."*

# Today I...

**Boost Yourself Tip:**

**Beckie Sanderson - Miss Digital Media**
**www.missdigitalmedia.co.uk**

*"Use technology and apps to automate your marketing and communications. Such as social media scheduling tools, automated email marketing, and messenger bots."*

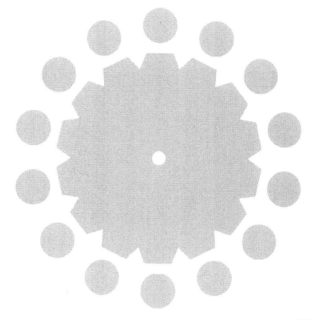

# Today I...

**Boost Yourself Tip:**

**Ginny Marsh - Gorgeous You Photography**
**www.gorgeousyouphotography.co.uk**

*"Try different poses in selfie mode with the self-timer on your phone
and see what the most flattering shapes are for your unique body shape.
Confidence comes from getting good at something with practice."*

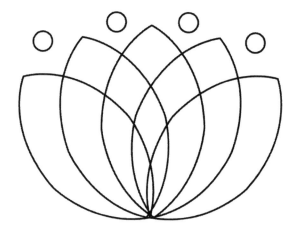

# Today I...

**Boost Yourself Tip:**

**Beckie Sanderson - Miss Digital Media**
**www.missdigitalmedia.co.uk**

*"The Canva platform is an excellent tool for your business and branding development, making design accessible to all, with a host of templates, formats, free and affordable content, you can add your own branding elements, colours and fonts, and quickly generate and repourpose content for your online marketing and print media."*

# Today I...

**Boost Yourself Tip:**

**Anna Murray Vanern Healing**
**www.everythingmakessensenow.wordpress.com**

*"Give yourself permission physically, mentally, emotionally,
and spiritually, to do something just for you."*

# Today I...

# Today I...

**Boost Yourself Tip:**

**Miki Maruko - Business Life Coaching**
**www.mikimaruko.com**

*"Your success starts with you believing in and trusting yourself.*
*Practice believing intentional thoughts about yourself and your business everyday and*
*taking small action steps from that place to build up your self-trust and belief*
*- from there, your success is inevitable."*

# Business Directory

**Alice Elliot**
**The Commenting Club**
www.thecommentingclub.co.uk
Facebook: @TheCommentingClub

**Anna Murray**
**Vanern Healing**
www.everythingmakessensenow.wordpress.com
Facebook: @VanernHealing

**Annabelle Antão-Bithrey**
**House of Colour Longfield**
www.houseofcolour.co.uk/find-a-stylist/profile/5641
Facebook: @hoclongfield

**Beckie Sanderson**
**Miss Digital Media**
www.missdigitalmedia.co.uk
Facebook: @missdigitalmedia
Instagram: @missdigitalmedia
Facebook Group: missdigitalmediaclassroom

**Becky Clarke Becky Clarke**
**Tarot Reader and Astrologer**
www.thebeckyclarke.co.uk
Facebook: @thebeckyclarke

**Barbara Edwards**
**BeCoached**
**www.becoached.ie**
Facebook: @becoachedBE

**Bettina Siddiqi**
**BusyB Solutions**
www.busy-bsolutions.com
www.linkedin.com/in/bettinasiddiqi-marketing/

**Bridget Daley**
**Parents in Biz**
www.parentsinbiz.co.uk
Instagram: @parentsinbiz

**Chris Melvile**
**Transform with Chris M**
www.transformwithchrism.com
Facebook: @TransformWithChrisM

**Carla Watkins**
**Business & Branding Photography**
www.carlawatkins.com
Instagram: @catalystcarla

**Emma Whalley**
**Gossip Gals**
www.gossipgalsnetworking.com
Facebook: @GossipGalsBusiness

**Emma York**
**Fresh Approach Digital**
www.freshapproachdigital.co.uk
Instagram: @freshapproachdigital

**Esther Ocampo**
**IPA Group**
**& The Monday Morning Marketing Podcast**
www.ipagroup.co | Twitter.com: @IPAGROUPEN
www.themondaymorningmarketing.com
Twitter.com: @mmmarketingcom

**Faye Cox**
**Faye Cox Coaching**
www.fayecoxcoaching.co.uk
Instagram: @fayecoxcoaching

**Francesca Wynn**
**Network Inspired**
www.network-inspired.co.uk
Facebook: @NetworkInspiration

Ginny Marsh
**Gorgeous You Photography
& Gorgeous You Coaching**
www.gorgeousyouphotography.co.uk
www.gorgeousyoucoaching.com
Instagram: @gorgeousyoucoaching
Instagram: @ginnymarshphotography

Halima Keshav (Mindful Coach/Reflexologist)
**Beautiful Sole Therapies**
www.beautifulsole.co.uk
Instagram: @beautifulsole_1

Helen Spina
**Gem Holistics & Helen's Gift shop**
Facebook: @Gemholistics
Facebook group: 217280975460961

Jane Singleton
**Jane Singleton Wellbeing**
www.janesingletonreflexology.co.uk
Instagram: @jane_singleton_wellbeing

Jen Parker
**Job Done Digital**
www.jobdonedigital.com
Instagram: @jobdonedigital

Katie Earl
**Katie Earl Editing**
www.katie-earl-editing.co.uk
Facebook: @katieearl.editing

Katie McGreal
**Solas Relaxation agus Relax Kids**
www.solasrelaxation.com
Facebook:@solasrelaxation

**Katie Spreadbury**
**OrangeSheep Research Ltd**
www.orangesheepresearch.co.uk
Facebook: @orangesheepresearch

**Kelly-Anne Geary**
**Tweak2Peak Lifestyle Coaching**
www.tweak2peaklifestylecoaching.co.uk.
Facebook: @Tweak2PeakLifestyleCoaching

**Lee McQueen**
**Small Biz & Marketing Coach**
www.lee-mcqueen.com
Instagram: @iamleemcqueen

**Lisa Gillbe**
**Lisa Gillbe Style Consultancy**
www.lisagillbestyle.com
Instagram: @lisegillbestylist

**Lisa Lomas**
**Lisa Lomas Therapies**
Facebook Group: Lisa Lomas Therapies Community
Instagram: @lisalomastherapies

**Lisa Talbot**
**Lisa Talbot Personal Stylist**
www.lisatalbot.co.uk
Instagram: @lisatalbot1

**Lynn Rees**
**Lynn Rees Virtual Assistant**
**www.lynnreesva.co.uk**
Facebook: @lynnreesva

**Nikki Sawyer**
**Sentient - Fear to Freedom For Mums**
www.nikkisawyer.co.uk
Facebook: @nikki.sawyertofeel
Facebook Group: Feartofreedomformums

**Nisha Harichandran**
**Bohem Notes**
www.bohemiancrossing.blog
Instagram @bohemnotes

**Magdalena Kuraczowska**
**FAB Consulting Agency**
www.femaleandbusiness.com
Instagram: @fab.mentor

**Maya Saric**
**SharpShine Copy**
www.Sharpshinecopy.com
Facebook: @maja.saricbilamilosevic

**Melanie Boylan**
**STOMP Social Media Training Ltd**
www.stomp.ie
Instagram: @melanie_boylan

**Miki Maruko**
**Business Life Coaching**
www.mikimaruko.com
@iammikimaruko

**Rachel Whiteside-Blaxter**
**Mindfulness Financial Planning**
www.mindfulnessfp.co.uk
Instagram: @mindfulnessfp

**Samantha Houghton**
**Memoir Mentor and Ghostwriter**
www.samanthahoughton.co.uk
Facebook: @TheInspiringWriter

**Samantha Slater**
**The Time & Money Coach**
www.samanthajaneslater.com
Facebook: @SamanthaJaneSlater
Facebook Group: TheFemaleBusinessOwnersMastermind

**Sarah Scarfe**
**Sarah Scarfe Marketing Ltd**
www.sarahscarfe.com
@SarahScarfeMKTG

**Sheree Owen**
**Sheree Owen Sales Strategist**
www.shereeowensalesstrategist.co.uk
linkedin.com/in/shereeowen

THE SALES STRATEGIST
Authentic Selling Expert

**Shona Chambers**
**Shona Chambers Marketing**
**& Self Employed Club**
www.shonachambersmarketing.co.uk
Instagram: @shonachambersmarketing

**Soaad Patel**
**Ayeshas Attire**
www.ayeshasattire.com
Facebook: @ayeshasattireonlineclothingstore

**Yuki Solle**
**Cultivate Life**
www.cultivatethelife.com
Instagram: @cultivatethelife

CULTIVATE
life

# Contact Miss Digital Media

Please get in touch: if you need help to develop your own ideal client info sheets, or would like to give some feedback on the Boost Yourself Journal, please find Miss Digital Media on Facebook, leave a review, post or comment using the Hashtags **#BoostYourselfJournal #Idealclient**

## Join my Facebook Group!

If you're a coach, consultant or creative who is looking to improve your marketing then I'd love to invite you to my Facebook group, **'Boost your Skills, Boost your Brand with Miss Digital Media.'** You'll get access to a ton of training and resources to help you to up-level your marketing skills and increase your visibility online - even if you're a complete technophobe!

## Book a FREE 1-2-1 Consultation today!

- Need a logo design?
- Stuck with your branding?
- Want training to boost your digital skills?
- Baffled by blogs or wondering about your website?
- Don't have a clue what to post on social media?
- Need help with self-publishing books or ebooks?

I'm here to help!

Book a video call with me so we can discuss your business, your project, and your needs, and develop a plan that will provide you with the resources, information, and advice to move forward.

## Get in touch!

- **Miss Digital Media**
- **www.missdigitalmedia.co.uk**
- **beckie@missdigitalmedia.co.uk**
- Instagram: **@missdigitalmedia**
- Facebook: **@missdigitalmedia**
- Facebook Group: **@missdigitalmediaclassroom**

# MiSS DiGiTAL MEDiA

Printed in Poland
by Amazon Fulfillment
Poland Sp. z o.o., Wrocław

80217796R00116